How Do We Feel and Touch?

Carol Ballard

RSVP

**RAINTREE
STECK-VAUGHN**
P U B L I S H E R S
The Steck-Vaughn Company

Austin, Texas

How Your Body Works

How Do Our Eyes See?

How Do Our Ears Hear?

How Do We Taste and Smell?

How Do We Feel and Touch?

How Do We Think?

How Do We Move?

Published by Raintree Steck-Vaughn Publishers, an imprint of Steck-Vaughn Company

Library of Congress Cataloging-in-Publication Data
Ballard, Carol.
How do we feel and touch? / Carol Ballard.
p.   cm.—(How your body works)
Includes bibliographical references and index.
Summary: A basic introduction to how our bodies feel sensations, exploring such topics as skin receptors, pressure, hot and cold, and pain.
ISBN 0-8172-4739-4
1. Touch—Juvenile literature.
[1. Touch. 2. Senses and sensation.]
I. Title. II. Series.
QP451.B35   1998
612.8'8—dc21   96-3261

Printed in Italy. Bound in the United States.
1 2 3 4 5 6 7 8 9 0 02 01 00 99 98

Picture acknowledgments
The author and publishers thank the following for use of their photographs:
Action-Plus 25 (top); Allsport 23 (top); Bubbles *title page*, 18, 23 (bottom), 25; Zul/Chapel Studios 5 (top), 12, 14, 16, 19, 21; Bruce Coleman 28; Greg Evans 4, 20; Chris Fairclough 6, 27; Impact 5 (bottom); NHPA 10; Oxford Scientific Films 29; Science Photo Library 26. Illustrators: Kevin Jones Associates and Michael Courtney

Contents

Touching 4

Inside the Skin 6

How Do Receptors Work? 8

Light Touch 10

Make a Feely Box 12

How Sensitive Are You? 14

Pressure 16

Itch and Tickle 18

Hot and Cold 20

Pain 22

Controlling Pain 24

When Things Go Wrong 26

Animals and Plants 28

Glossary 30

Books to Read 31

Index 32

Touching

Our sense of touch is important. We use it to collect information about the world around us. Imagine you are given something you have never seen before. You could find out about it just by touching it. Is it hard like metal or rough like the bark of a tree? Is it sharp and prickly like a porcupine or soft like a kitten's fur?

▲ Our skin feels cold in winter. This boy is blowing into his hands to warm them.

◄ The tree bark feels rough and scratchy under this girl's hands.

4

Our sense of touch helps to keep us safe. For example, if you put your hand on something very hot, you react instantly by pulling your hand away before it gets burned.

▲ These girls are wearing dresses made of velvet. Velvet feels very soft and smooth.

Blind people rely on their sense of touch. Many things that they use, such as knobs on stoves, have raised bumps for them to feel rather than see.

This book tells you about your sense of touch and how it works.

Dry sand and wet sand feel ▶ different to the touch.

Inside the Skin

Skin forms a protective covering. It stops harmful things from getting into the body. It helps control body temperature and the amount of water lost through sweating. **Receptor** cells in the skin allow us to feel the objects we touch.

▲

The outer layer of skin is much thicker on our feet than anywhere else on our bodies.

There are two main layers of skin. The outer layer is called the **epidermis**. It is made up of dead cells, which get worn away by our everyday activities, so it is constantly being replaced with new cells from the inner layer.

◄ Sunlight contains ultraviolet light, which can be dangerous to our skin. To protect us our skin makes extra **pigment** — we develop a suntan.

The inner layer is called the **dermis**. It contains **capillaries**, nerves, and hairs. It also contains sweat glands and **ducts**, which carry sweat to the surface of the skin. Receptor cells are also in the dermis. Some are near the surface; others are deeply buried. **Nerves** connect the receptor cells to the brain.

If you could look inside your skin ▼ with a microscope, it would look something like this.

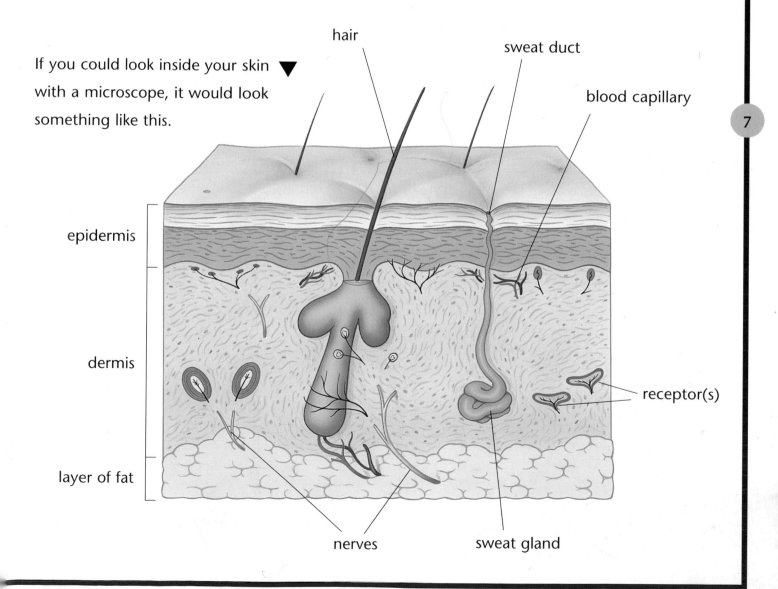

hair

sweat duct

blood capillary

epidermis

dermis

receptor(s)

layer of fat

nerves

sweat gland

How Do Receptors Work?

There are special types of receptors for touch, pressure, pain, hot, and cold. Each receptor can only respond to its own special feeling. For example, if you put your hand into warm water, the heat receptors will respond but the cold receptors will not.

▲
Messages from receptor cells travel to the upper-back part of the brain.

Some sensations involve more than one type of receptor. If you pick up something hot and sharp, both heat and pain receptors will respond.

When a receptor is **stimulated**, it responds by sending a message along nerves to the brain. The brain knows where the message came from, so it can tell exactly where the feeling is. It decides whether action is necessary and may send a message to the muscles telling them to move part of your body. This all happens in a fraction of a second, so it seems as if you feel as soon as you touch.

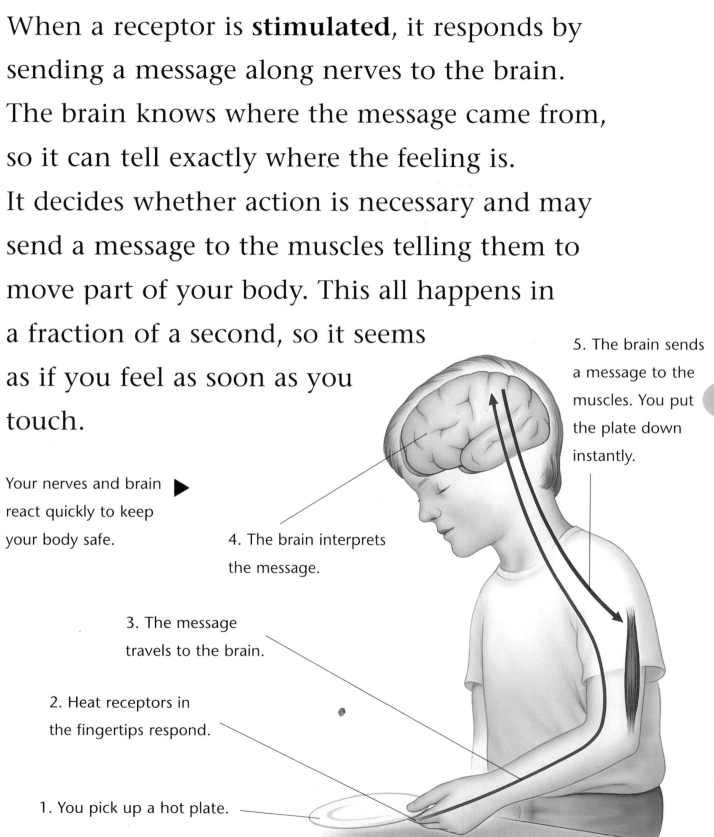

Your nerves and brain ▶ react quickly to keep your body safe.

5. The brain sends a message to the muscles. You put the plate down instantly.

4. The brain interprets the message.

3. The message travels to the brain.

2. Heat receptors in the fingertips respond.

1. You pick up a hot plate.

Light Touch

If something touches you lightly, it makes contact with your skin but does not press hard. The shape of your skin does not change, and the feeling usually lasts for only a short time.

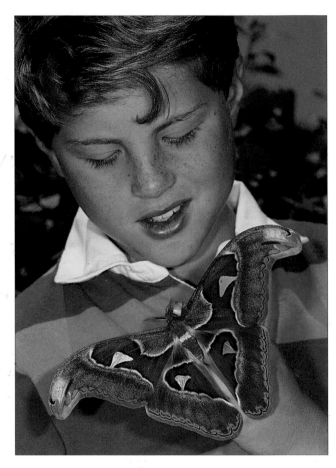

▲

Even though the moth's wings are delicate, this boy can feel them brushing lightly over his hand.

There are different types of light-touch receptors. The most common are free nerve endings. Others have a tiny disk attached to them or are surrounded by an egg-shaped protective case. Most receptors lie at the join between the two skin layers.

Some light-touch receptors cluster around the ends of hairs and respond to movement of the hair. This means you can feel something that touches your hair though it does not touch your skin.

Some parts of the body have many light-touch receptors, so they are very **sensitive**. Other parts do not have as many, so they are less sensitive.

hair

hair root

receptors

There are different types of light-touch receptors. ▶ ▼

▲

The receptors around a hair can detect very tiny hair movements.

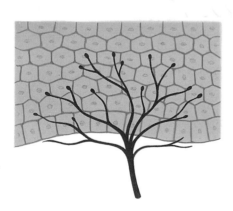

Some receptors have free nerve endings.

Some receptors have egg-shaped capsules.

Some receptors are like flat disks.

Make a Feely Box

How much can you find out just by feeling things? You can use a feely box to find out.

You will need a cardboard box with a lid. Mark and cut two holes in one side, big enough to put your hands through. Decorate the outside of the box if you want to.

▲
Objects that could go inside a feely box

◄ These children are trying to find out what is inside the feely box.

Choose some small objects to put into the box. You could choose things with different textures, for example, a piece of bark, a pebble, and a spiky pinecone. You could choose things that have different shapes. You might choose a smooth object such as a plastic ruler or pencil case, or long flexible objects such as drinking straws or yarn. Or you could make a collection of soft or round objects.

Put the objects in the box and put the lid back on. Ask friends to put their hands through the holes and pick up one object at a time. Keep a record of the objects they can and cannot identify. See if they find it easier to detect objects of different textures or of different shapes.

Person \ Object	Bark	Seashell	Pebble	Eraser
Mark	✔	✗	✔	✗
Javed	✗	✔	✗	✔
Susan	✔	✔		
Ravinda	✔			
Ellen	✔			

▲ Record your results on a table like this.

13

How Sensitive Are You?

Are some parts of your body more sensitive to touch than others? Try this activity with a friend to find out. You will need a washable felt pen and a fine bristle from an old hairbrush.

Decide which parts of the body you want to test. The palm and back of your hand and the top and sole of your foot are ideal, but you could try other parts too.

◀ These children are trying to find out which is more sensitive: the palm of the hand or the back of the hand.

Mark a pattern of twenty small dots on the area to be tested. The person being tested must not look as you gently touch one of the dots with the bristle. Note when they feel the bristle and when they do not. Then do the same for other parts of the body.

Look at your results to see which part of the body was most sensitive and which was least sensitive.

▲

If you draw a regular pattern of dots, it is much easier to keep track of the ones you have already tested.

15

When you have finished your test, draw ▶ a bar chart to show your results.

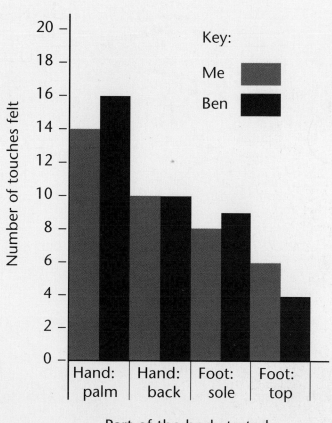

Key:

Me

Ben

Number of touches felt

Part of the body tested

Pressure

If you press something hard, your skin will be pushed in. This is different than just touching something lightly, and it is detected by different receptors. The feeling of pressure usually lasts longer and is spread over a larger area than the feeling of light touch.

▲
We can often feel the sensation of pressure long after the object that caused it has been taken away.

▲
The hand in this picture is resting lightly on the skin. The skin is not pushed out of shape. There is no pressure.

▲
The hand in this picture is pressing hard on the skin. Look at the way the skin is dented. There is pressure.

Most pressure receptors lie inside the dermis of the skin. Pressure receptors are usually larger than light-touch receptors and are surrounded by a capsule. They measure tiny changes in pressure, rather than the actual pressure.

Pressure receptors also pick up **vibrations.** Some are sensitive to very fast vibrations and others to slow vibrations. Like light-touch receptors, some pressure receptors cluster around hair shafts and pick up hair movements.

B

B receptors pick up fast vibrations

A

capsule

C

capsule

nerve endings

nerve endings

Receptors **A** and **C** pick up slow vibrations

These receptors all detect changes in pressure.

Itch and Tickle

Part of the body usually starts to itch when nerves in the skin are stimulated over and over again. Itches occur particularly around the eyes and nose.

Itches can also be caused by chemicals. When bitten by an insect, your body responds by releasing chemicals. These chemicals make your skin feel itchy. Some illnesses, such as chickenpox, also cause this sort of itch.

▲
Scratching a chemical itch will only make it worse.

◄ Treating an insect bite with the right ointment can keep it from itching.

When you scratch an itch, it usually feels better right away. However, if it is a chemical itch, scratching can make it worse. The scratching irritates the skin, so more chemicals are released and the skin itches even more.

Many people are ticklish on the feet, the palms of the hands, or the back of the neck. A tickle is caused by the same type of **stimulus** as an itch, although it is usually more gentle and moves across the surface of the skin.

Light, gentle movements ▶ can tickle a lot.

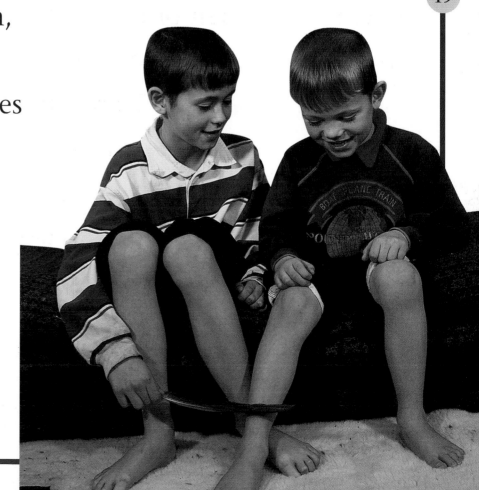

Hot and Cold

We cannot tell exactly how hot or cold something is, we can only compare the temperature with that of our skin.

We have two different types of temperature receptors. Heat receptors respond to things that are hotter than skin temperature. Cold receptors respond to things that are colder than skin temperature. The heat and cold receptors are free nerve endings. They lie at the top of the dermis, just below the epidermis.

▲ A thermometer can tell us the exact temperature. Our bodies can only compare the temperature with that of our skin.

◄ We cover and protect our bodies in the winter, but our faces are exposed all the time. The face is less sensitive to cold than the rest of the body.

Heat and cold receptors are not spread evenly throughout the body. They are clustered together in hot spots, which respond to heat, and cold spots, which respond to cold. The lips have hot spots and cold spots so they can detect both heat and cold. Our teeth are much more sensitive to cold than to heat.

This girl has her left hand in cold water and ▶ her right hand in hot water. If she then puts both hands into warm water, her brain will get confusing messages. Right-hand receptors will send a "cold" message and left-hand receptors will send a "hot" message. She will find it hard to tell how warm the water actually is.

Pain

Pain is a warning signal to the body about something harmful, dangerous, or unpleasant. It makes us do something to remove ourselves from the danger before any serious damage is done. It is important that we notice pain whenever it occurs so that we can react.

There are several types of pain. Some pain can be sharp and pricking; other pain can be a slow burning or a deep ache.

There are different types of pain. A broken leg will ▶ probably feel like a deep ache. A thumb hit by a hammer will probably feel as if it is on fire!

22

We feel pain when our pain receptors respond to something. Pain receptors are free nerve endings. They occur in every part of the body except the intestines and the brain. Some parts of the body are much more sensitive than others to pain. Pricking the skin of your finger with a needle will cause pain, but the same needle used for an injection into a muscle will cause less pain.

▲ This athlete has stopped running because she has a painful injury.

Cleaning a cut or a graze ▶ may hurt more than the injury itself, but it will prevent **infection** and help healing.

Controlling Pain

There are many ways of trying to control pain. Some medicines, such as painkillers, can help to reduce pain. They do not take away the cause of the pain. They just alter the brain's reaction to the pain so that you are less aware of it.

▲
Before anesthetics were invented, doctors tried other ways of putting patients to sleep!

In the hospital and at the dentist's, **anesthetic** is given to control pain. Dentists inject anesthetic into the gum to make it numb before filling a tooth. A general anesthetic puts a patient to sleep before an operation.

There are ways of reducing pain that do not rely on drugs. The Chinese system of acupuncture has been used for more than three thousand years. Special needles are inserted carefully into the body, in exactly the right places. The person is unable to feel any pain, and doctors can carry out an operation. Nobody knows exactly why acupuncture works, but it may make the brain produce its own painkilling chemicals.

▲
Spraying a local anesthetic onto an injury will stop the pain, but the athlete may make the injury worse by playing on.

25

◄ Many dentists use a local anesthetic to make part of the mouth numb before they start any treatment.

When Things Go Wrong

Pain is not always felt in the same place as the injury or disease that causes it. For example, people suffering from some types of heart disease often feel pain in the left arm. This type of pain is called referred pain.

▲ Like this pirate, people with only one leg can sometimes still feel a pain in the missing leg.

◀ This man suffering from heart disease may feel pain in his left arm as well as in his chest.

Some people who have had a leg cut off still feel pain in it, even though it is not there. This is called phantom pain. Doctors think it happens when nerve endings that connected the limb to the brain are stimulated. The brain thinks it is getting a message from the limb itself.

A few people cannot feel pain at all. This can cause many problems. Pain is really a signal warning us of something that may damage our bodies. Without this warning system, children who cannot feel pain have to be very careful. They could burn a hand and not even notice. They have to check their bodies regularly to make sure there is no damage.

If a child who cannot feel pain falls off ▶ a bike, he or she must check carefully to find out if there are any injuries.

Animals and Plants

Other living things can feel things in the world around them.

Sharks have hundreds of tiny holes in their faces and along the sides of their bodies. These can detect very small electrical signals that other creatures give off, and small movements in the water. Sharks use the electrical signals and the water movements to pinpoint their prey.

▲
Cats use their whiskers to detect tiny movements in the air. They use them to pinpoint where something is.

◄ A shark can pick up tiny electrical signals and water movements.

Snakes have very sensitive heat detectors. Special holes on the sides of their heads can pick up the heat given off by warm-blooded animals. This helps the snake to locate its prey, even if it cannot see it or hear it.

Some plants are sensitive to touch. The Venus fly trap relies on touch to catch its food. When an insect lands on the end of a leaf, leaf hairs detect the movement. This triggers the leaf to snap shut, trapping the insect inside.

Leaves being touched

Leaves after being touched

▲ This sensitive plant called a mimosa curls up its leaves if you touch it.

Glossary

anesthetic A substance that blocks feelings of pain.

capillaries Very small blood vessels.

cell One of the millions of tiny building blocks that make up your body.

dermis The inner layer of the skin.

ducts Tubes in the body that carry fluid.

epidermis The outer layer of the skin.

infection Illness caused by germs that get into the body.

nerves Cells that carry messages to and from the brain.

pigment A substance present in the body that produces color.

receptor A cell that reacts to a stimulus, sending a message to the brain.

sensitive Quick to feel and react to touch.

stimulus A change that affects a receptor.

vibration A tiny back-and-forth movement.

Books to Read

Fowler, Allan. *Feeling Things.* (Rookie Read-about Science.) Danbury, CT: Children's Press, 1991.

Morris, Neil. *Feel! A Fun Book of Touch.* (Fun Books of Learning.) Minneapolis, MN: Lerner Group, 1991.

Pluckrose, Henry. *Exploring Our Senses: Touching.* Milwaukee, WI: Gareth Stevens, Inc., 1995.

Rowe, Julian. *Feel & Touch.* Danbury, CT: Children's Press, 1993.

Index

acupuncture 25
anesthetic 24, 25
animals 28

blind people 5
body temperature 6
brain 7, 8, 9, 23, 24, 25, 27

capillaries 7

dermis 6, 7, 17, 20

epidermis 6, 20

feely box 12–13

hairs 7, 11, 17

itch 18, 19

muscles 9

nerve endings 10, 20
nerves 7, 9, 18

pain 22, 23, 24, 25, 26, 27
    insensitivity to 27
    phantom pain 26, 27
    referred pain 26
painkillers 24, 25

receptors 6, 7, 8, 9, 16, 20
    cold receptors 8, 20, 21
    heat receptors 8, 20, 21
    pain receptors 8, 23
    pressure receptors 8, 16, 17
    touch receptors 10, 11, 17

scratching 8, 19
sensation 8
sensitivity test 14–15
skin 6, 7, 10, 11, 16, 17, 18, 19
skin temperature 20

tickle 19

vibrations 17